"I was born in a family whose roots are deep in the tradition and practice of the Way of Tea; my life, like those of my ancestors, has been imbued with its spirit.

"I have toured the world for more than a quarter of a century with the goal 'Peace through sharing a bowl of tea.' This peace can be spread by offering a bowl of tea to another. The simple act of serving tea and receiving it with gratitude is the basis for the way of life called *Chado*, the Way of Tea."

—Soshitsu Sen, Grand Master XV
Urasenke School of Tea

TEA LIFE, TEA MIND

The four Japanese characters on the endpapers, in calligraphy by the author, have the following meanings, reading from left to right and front to back: harmony, respect, purity, tranquility.

SOSHITSU SEN XV

TEA LIFE, TEA MIND

New York · WEATHERHILL · *Tokyo*

Translated and edited in the Foreign Affairs Section, Urasenke Foundation, Ogawa Teranouchi agaru, Kamikyo-ku, Kyoto 602, Japan.

First edition, 1979
Tenth printing, 1995

Published by Weatherhill, Inc., of New York and Tokyo, with editorial offices at 568 Broadway, Suite 705, N.Y., N.Y. 10012.

LCC Card Number 79-10763   ISBN 0-8348-0412-6

The motif of the gold and silk brocade shown on the cover is a Chinese phoenix, *ho*, amid clouds of fortune, *un*, and is the graphic representation of the author's Buddhist name, Hounsai.

TO

MY FATHER, MY MOTHER

AND MY WIFE

CONTENTS

PREFACE

THE SIMPLE ACT of serving tea and receiving it with gratitude is the basis for a way of life called *Chado,* the Way of Tea. When serving a bowl of tea in conformity with Tea etiquette, a cultural synthesis of wide scope and high ideals is brought into play with aspects of religion, morality, aesthetics, philosophy, discipline, and social relations.

The student of Tea learns to arrange things, to understand timing and interludes, to appreciate social graces, and to apply all of these to daily experience. These things are all brought to bear in the simple process of serving and receiving a bowl of tea, and are done with a single purpose—to realize tranquility of mind in communion with one's fellow men within our world. It is in this that the Way of Tea has meaning for today.

With a bowl of tea, peace can truly spread. The peacefulness from a bowl of tea may be shared and become the foundation of a way of life.

I was born in a family whose roots are deep in the tradition and practice of the Way of Tea; my life, like those of my ancestors, has been imbued with its spirit. My earliest memories include the tearooms of my home, tea utensils I played with, tea lessons with my father, and the endless round of guests received with a bowl of frothy green tea. In 1964, I succeeded my father as head of the family and became the fifteenth-generation Grand Master of the Urasenke School of Tea, leader of more than two million students of the Urasenke tradition. It is my own life and thoughts that I offer to you now.

I am grateful to Dr. Herman Kahn, founder, president, and director of the Hudson Institute, for allowing me to include his interview with me, which appears in the Appendix. Also, I would like to thank the staff of the Foreign Affairs Section of the Urasenke Foundation for their translation and editing of my Japanese manuscript.

INTRODUCTION

A MONK ONCE ASKED his master, "No matter what lies ahead, what is the Way?" The master quickly replied, "The Way is your daily life." This concept is at the very center of the Way of Tea. The principles of the Way of Tea are directed toward all of one's existence, not just to the part that takes place in the tearoom. In practice, the test lies in meeting each occurrence of each day with a clear mind, in a composed state. In a sense, even one's smallest action is the Way of Tea. It is this that makes it just as significant today as when it began more than four hundred and fifty years ago.

The practice of drinking powdered green tea was brought to Japan by monks returning from their studies at the great Zen monasteries of twelfth-century China. For them tea served as an aid to meditation, as a medicine, and as a tool to propagate Zen. About two hundred years later it was drunk for completely different reasons, at tea-tasting contests accompanied by lavish banquets, with ostentatious displays of wealth and possessions, and the wagering of massive stakes. The participants at these contests seemed to have found in this glittering world of excess a means to escape from their uncertain times.

At the end of the fifteenth century, the practice of serving tea was studied by the Zen priest Murata Shuko (1422–1502). He was knowledgeable about the procedures of tea service in the shogun's court and was a disciple of the famous Zen priest Ikkyu (1394–1481), who encouraged his practice. His manner of serving tea reflected his Zen background. In contrast to the spacious rooms and elegant Chinese utensils generally used at that time, he preferred to serve tea in a small room with a minimum number of utensils, many of domestic origin. In this way Shuko found that the serving of tea was more than merely a ritual of refined elegance.

The practice of drinking tea was also developing among members of the merchant class. In these circumstances as well, it acquired new characteristics. As opposed to the solemnity of the shogun's court, the serving of tea by men of commerce had a much livelier air. Many of the merchant tea masters were deeply involved in Zen. Although the atmosphere of their gatherings differed from that of Shuko's, the foundation was the same.

One of the most important men to emerge from this group was Takeno Jo-o (1502–55). During his life, he began to develop the concept of an entirely new style of tea practice, *wabi* tea. This is a style of tea practiced in a small rustic hut with utensils of a quiet, humble character. Modest and without ostentation, it combines the aesthetics of Zen with the egalitarianism of democracy. This style was later to be fully developed by Jo-o's disciple, Sen Rikyu.

Sen Rikyu (1522–91) began his studies with Jo-o at the age of nineteen. Like Jo-o, he had grown up in a merchant's family and was a resident of the port of Sakai, near Osaka. To recount his personal history and the contributions he made to the practice of Tea would take volumes. Suffice it to say here that it is Rikyu's organization and blending of the many styles of Tea practiced up to his time, along with their philosophy, procedures, and histories, that we today know as the Way of Tea.

Rikyu identified the spirit of the Way of Tea with the four basic principles of harmony, respect, purity, and tranquility. These four principles underlie all the practical rules of Tea and represent at the same time its highest ideals.

"Harmony" is the result of the interaction of the host and guest, the food served, and the utensils used with the flowing rhythms of nature. It reflects both the evanescence of all things and the unchanging in the changing. The host interacts with the guest, both thinking of one another as if their roles were reversed. Before tea is served, the host will offer a sweet to the guest, or often a light meal. In both cases, what is served should be appropriate to the season. Utensils should be in harmony with each other and the mood and theme of the tea gathering. The close correspondence with nature further focuses our attention on the transient quality of a tea gathering. The principle of harmony means to be free of pretensions, walking the path of moderation, becoming neither heated nor cold, and never forgetting the attitude of humility.

"Respect" is the sincerity of heart that liberates us for an open relationship with the immediate environment, our fellow human beings, and nature, while recognizing the innate dignity of each. Respect gives structure to a tea gathering and orders the exchanges among the participants, primarily through the standardized tea etiquette. But in a much broader sense, without regard for appearances, this principle presses us to look deeply into the hearts of all people we meet and at the things in our environment. It is then that we realize our kinship with all the world around us.

"Purity," through the simple act of cleaning, is an important part of a tea gathering—in the preparation beforehand, the actual service of tea, and, after the guests have left, the storing away of the utensils and the final closing of the tearoom. Such actions as clearing the dust from the room and the dead leaves from the garden path all represent clearing the "dust of the world," or the worldly attachments, from one's heart and mind. It is then, after putting aside material concerns, that people and things can be perceived in their truest state. The act of cleaning thus enables one to sense the pure and sacred essence of things, man, and nature.

When the host is cleaning and arranging the areas that the guests will occupy, he is establishing order also within himself; this order is essential. As he attends to the details of the tearoom and garden path, he is no less attending to his own consciousness and to the state of mind in which he will serve his guest.

"Tranquility," an aesthetic concept unique to Tea, comes with the constant practice of the first three principles of harmony, respect, and purity in our everyday lives. Sitting alone, away from the world, at one with the rhythms of nature, liberated from attachments to the material world and bodily comforts, purified and sensitive to the sacred essence of all that is around, a person making and drinking tea in contemplation approaches a sublime state of tranquility. But, strange to say, this tranquility will deepen even further when another person enters the microcosm of the tearoom and joins the host in contemplation over a bowl of tea. That we can find a lasting tranquility within our own selves in the company of others is the paradox.

TEA LIFE, TEA MIND

MASTERING THE WAY

A man spends his entire life sitting in meditation at the peak of a great mountain. His deepest gratitude is for being able to sit in such a manner. Without such thankfulness, whatever we may do will amount to nothing. —This is the attitude taught me by my father, the Urasenke Grand Tea Master before me.

IT IS OFTEN JOKINGLY REMARKED that not blood but tea runs in my veins. This may not be an overstatement; it does seem to me I was raised more on tea than on milk. As a child, my play areas and private living space always included a tearoom. I often played in the *tokonoma,* or decorative alcove, where a scroll is hung and a simple flower arrangement placed. Or I would mischievously stick my fingers in the brazier or hearth, stirring up the ash that had been carefully prepared to ventilate the fire used to heat water for tea.

As prescribed by tradition, at the age of six on the sixth day of the sixth month, I began tea lessons. The first part of my training was to become familiar with the utensils. I was allowed to hold tea bowls and bamboo ladles freely. My parents were careful not to dampen my young spirit and at first only gradually introduced me to the proper procedures, beginning with a simple bow and correcting things gradually as time passed. At the same time, however, I was quite forcefully taught that objects are not to be treated carelessly, and that I must be responsible for my own actions. Wisely, my parents did not try to teach too much at one time.

Once my lessons with my father began, it was a rule that no one else was allowed to enter the room. Even my mother had to remain outside. Nevertheless, she sat on the other side of the papered sliding doors and listened carefully to everything I was taught. When the lesson was over, she would meet me outside the room and ask if I had understood everything my father had said. If I was the least bit unsure, she patiently explained it to me again. In her own way she, too, was my teacher. For example, though she herself never saw me during my formal lessons, she could keenly sense how I walked by the sounds that I made, and unreservedly criticized my manner of walking, although my father had not mentioned anything about it.

Somehow, I resolved, I had to master the manner of walking properly. Holding a small ceramic brazier filled with ash in front of me, I practiced walking barefoot up and down a long hallway. Though the brazier was quite heavy, I was careful not to forget my form. Rather than concentrate so much on a certain style of walking, instead I had to walk naturally. Through this exercise, my entire body was brought into balance.

I have very few childhood recollections of having played with my father. On chance occasions when we would pass each other in the hall, for example, he would pat my head and say, "Everything going well?" Another opportunity I can remember is when my father left his work to go into the garden to do exercises that he had devised to relieve his body of stiffness. He often had to appraise tea utensils, writing his endorsement of them in his best calligraphy, tasks that I now realize leave one's whole body exhausted. If I came upon him in the garden, we would play catch or some other game. He must have been tired, but he always smiled brightly when we played.

While he was a wonderful father, he was at the same time an extremely stern man. If I tried to lean on him for help during my studies, he would push me away. Each time I was cast off, a lesson was learned, not just memorized. Although my father was neither sharp-tongued nor wordy in his instructions, it was as though he was telling me that what I tried to memorize would soon be forgotten, but whatever I learned with my own body would remain with me for a lifetime. It was not until much later that I fully realized the important lesson that he, in his silence, had taught me.

During my practice sessions, I always had to remain aware of my future, with its position and responsibilities. The necessity of this attitude was particularly impressed on me in one memorable incident. As my lessons progressed, I had begun to receive instruction from one of the senior teachers, a resident tea instructor who had achieved a certain degree of accomplishment and assisted my father. But I had the rather easygoing notion that, because my father was usually about, I should be taught by him all the time. One day I approached him with the question of why he could not give me more individual instruction. He said nothing. By the look on his face I could tell I was in trouble.

He told me to follow him to the room where a wooden statue of Sen Rikyu is enshrined. He made me sit before the altar and pay my respects to my ancestors. Then he reprimanded me for taking my training so lightly.

"Just because you were born to this house does not mean that you will become its master effortlessly. You must, from the start, be strict and severe in developing the Way for yourself. To that end, although the man who stands before you is your father, in these things I am not your father but the Grand Tea Master, practicing and training in the Way of Tea. Simply stated, as long as you pursue this path, I am your teacher. You take advantage of the fact that I am your father and ask me why I do not give you instruction. If you truly want to learn, come and ask me properly as a student requesting instruction from a teacher."

At that moment I saw him not as my father but as a great master of the Way. From then on, whenever he was available, I asked him, in the proper manner, for instruction and received it; and though we were father and son, in things pertaining to my learning, the new relationship of teacher and disciple was born.

One very important teaching of my father's was that it was a terrible offense to treat inanimate objects without respect or to release one's ill disposition on them. He was fond of telling me a story from his childhood by way of illustration. One day when my father was eight, he, his father, and his grandfather—the fourteenth-, thirteenth-, and twelfth-generation Grand Tea Masters respectively—visited a shrine in Tokyo where, in a special ceremony, they were to offer tea to the enshrined deities. His father promised him that if he performed the ceremony well, he could have anything he wished.

My father had been longing for a brass bugle and with the single intent to make it his, he executed his part beautifully, without mishap. His joy upon receiving the bugle was boundless and he took to blowing it with all his might. Perhaps he had only meant to rinse out the mouthpiece, but he soon found that it was also fun to shoot water in one end of the bugle and watch it come running out the other end. After a while, this little game ruined the instrument. "You performed the ceremony very well and as a result received a brass bugle. No matter how happy you were, it was bad to destroy it," his father reprimanded him. "If you truly aspire to the Way of Tea, it is a serious error to destroy things or treat them carelessly."

When I entered junior high school I was often taunted with, "Hey Sen! You're lucky, you know that? You won't have to choose a career because it's all decided for you. You don't have to set your sights on a university like the rest of us do. And even if you do go on to a university it doesn't really matter which one, does it?" I wished they could know how distinctly unlucky I felt, so I dragged a friend home with me and revealed everything to him about being in a position where I was expected to succeed in my father's work. After this, my friends gradually teased me less and even came to sympathize with me.

In junior high school, I participated in various sports because my parents had taught me that I should discipline my body. My first choice was horseback riding; I had enjoyed it as a child and considered riding more than a mere sport because, while it was extremely exhilarating, it also improved my posture. It is difficult to control a horse on the riding field or at the hurdles with only reins and inner strength, but the joy of acquiring this skill gave me a feeling of grandness beyond description.

Through riding and other sports I strengthened my body

and spirit. The practice of Tea is done mostly while sitting, and I am grateful to have found, through sports, my own balance of body and mind.

During the war years, my university studies were interrupted when I was drafted for military service, but I was able to return to school and graduated in 1946. At the same time I was acknowledged as the successor to my father, the Grand Tea Master, with the responsiblity of mastering the spiritual, scholastic, and technical aspects of the Way of Tea. The hurdle I now faced was the tradition that the Grand Tea Master also be a Zen priest, and so to prepare for my future position, I had to begin formal Zen training.

Goto Zuigan Roshi, an old acquaintance of my mother, had just become the head of Juko-in, a subtemple of Daitoku-ji temple, which was very near to our house and traditionally associated with Tea. It was a fortunate coincidence. After arrangements were made, I began my Zen training under him. I was very grateful to be able to study with such a noble, well-educated priest and outstanding man of Zen.

As my ancestors since the time of Rikyu had done, I surrendered my childhood name and entered the priesthood. After the initiation ceremonies I was given a new name signifying that I had become a true devotee of a life of Tea. At Goto Roshi's instruction, formal ceremonies were performed changing my childhood name of Masaoki to Hounsai, Phoenix Cloud. Finally after several additional name-bestowing ceremonies I commenced my Zen training at Juko-in with the name of Hounsai Genshusoko Koji.

Whenever I recall my arduous Rinzai Zen training under Goto Roshi, two of my teacher's oft-repeated sayings come to mind: "Become the inkstone that does not wear away no matter how many times it is rubbed," and "Demand. And then avidly seek to know."

In 1951 the opportunity arose for me to make a journey, my first, to the United States. At that time I received the koan *Shujinko,* or "Master," from Goto Roshi. It is an important koan based on the story of the Chinese monk Zuigan (after whom my teacher was named), who had carried on a dialogue with himself and had come to self-understanding.

The story goes that Zuigan devised a method of sitting alone in meditation on a rock.

"Shujinko," he called to himself.

"Yes, yes," he answered.

"Shujinko. Be warned against the deception of others around you. Aren't you doing something that will cause them to talk behind your back?"

And then he abruptly said, "Shujinko. Were you dozing just now?"

"No, I was not," was his reply.

One teaching of this koan is that we must have the confidence to say to ourselves, "No, I was not [dozing]." It is in this moment that we discover our true selves. In giving me this koan, Goto Roshi was reminding me of the principle inherent in *Shujinko:* that I must know myself, be my own master. Whether I was in Japan or overseas, or whether I was teaching Japanese or non-Japanese people, I was to remember my real search in life. My teacher apparently felt I had been granted an invaluable opportunity to look at myself from a distant shore, to understand my task in life, and to know my true self.

Preparing for my trip, I thought back over the development of the Way of Tea from its earliest beginnings in China to its taking root in Japan during the fifteenth and sixteenth centuries. In similar fashion, if I could introduce the Way of Tea to Americans, it might become an accepted practice overseas.

When going to America I received the endorsement of Brigadier General Dike of the Occupation Forces in Japan. He had come to understand Tea and knew that the Japanese were not barbarians; he also believed that Japanese democracy existed in the practice of Tea.

My father investigated every possible connection for me and wrote in his own hand a listing of those who had some tie with Urasenke. Like a young schoolboy sent on an important errand, I placed my precious list carefully in a large bag that I would never be parted from. In the bag, my mother also tucked in a small charm bag that she had sewn and, as a final safeguard against any unlikely event, a small diamond she had kept hidden away.

Thus, with the blessing of my family and a prayer in my heart that I could have the clearsightedness of Rikyu, I set off.

After innumerable hours by plane, I was deposited on the North American continent. I had very little confidence in my English, and my entire belongings consisted of my precious list, my charm, a travel permit issued by General MacArthur's headquarters, some clothes, and a check for a sum of money that was supposed to last for three months, amounting to an allotment of three dollars a day. Again, I felt like the little schoolboy and wondered how I would ever make it through the year. As a citizen of a defeated nation, of course, I did not expect to be treated as a guest, and I did not want to become too dependent. I had to be strict with myself in order to avoid becoming too easily accustomed to material comforts or, as I felt in those days, too "Westernized."

At the time, with the exception of a few men such as the famous Zen scholar Daisetz Suzuki, the Nobel Prize winner Hideki Yukawa, and the Christian educator Hachiro Yuasa, there were very few Japanese who went to the United States. Although my country had fought against the United States, I was eager to show the true heart of the Japanese people by preparing and sharing a bowl of tea with Americans.

I realized, however, that to see someone make a bowl of tea and listen to an explanation of it does not make the practice readily understandable. The environment in the United States is totally foreign to that which produced the Way of Tea, and it would have been wrong to think of propagating that spiritual practice as if it were export merchandise, like cameras.

Fortunately, even before World War II, there were Americans who had studied with my father or grandfather and some, my father told me, had even built tea huts. I resolved to make the fullest possible use of every opportunity to meet these dedicated people, through whose efforts there were eventually formed a number of organized groups of Tea teachers and students that now thrive in the United States.

In my year-long journey much goodwill and enthusiasm were generated, spurring me to make many more such trips to the American continent and other areas overseas during the next twenty-eight years.

Goto Roshi taught me to persevere in my course of action, all the while chastising me for going abroad so frequently. Jokingly, he said it was not for that reason that he had given me the name Phoenix Cloud. He advised, "You should be more cautious and not spread your wings so far. But, on the other hand, it may very well be your task in life to travel about. Each Grand Tea Master in the history of the Sen family has suffered the hardships of his age and I suppose you are meant to devote your life to these foreign pilgrimages.

"People such as yourself are, on the whole, blessed with good fortune from birth. You completed your education and experienced a war, and you should feel very grateful for such a broad background. Your father spread the Way of Tea to the entire nation. The important question is what to do now that it is your turn."

HOST AND GUEST

An unpainted, weathered gate, slightly ajar, is a guest's first sign of welcome to a tea gathering. Water has been sprinkled about, an indication of the host's readiness for his guests. The other guests arrive at about the same time, pass through the outer gate, and enter the entryway where they change their shoes and take off their wraps. After proceeding to a waiting room they are served small cups of hot water.

The guests then move to a sheltered waiting-arbor on the edge of a small garden. Quiet and unpretentious, modeled after a mountain trail, the simple stone pathway leads the guests through the compactly arranged trees, shrubs, and moss. The function of the garden is only to lead guests to the tea hut. In so doing the guests leave the mundane world and have an opportunity to relax and free their minds from worldly matters.

As the garden suggests a mountain trail, the tea hut suggests a simple mountain hermitage. Everyday materials, unpainted wooden posts and lintels, wattle walls, and thatched or bark roofs allow the structure to blend unobtrusively into the surroundings.

After being silently greeted by the host, the assembled guests one by one proceed along the path toward the tea hut. Near its entrance is a low stone basin; each guest stoops to rinse his hands and mouth in a symbolic act of purification. The guests proceed to the tea hut and enter by crawling through a small doorway.

Before the guests arrive, the host has hung a scroll in the alcove of the tea hut. Often the calligraphy of a Zen priest or tea master, it helps create a certain mood for the gathering.

In a freshly prepared bed of fine ash, a charcoal fire has been laid, incense is burned, and over the fire, the host has placed a kettle filled with water for making tea.

Upon entering, each guest appreciates the scroll, the fire, the arranged ash, the kettle, and any other utensils that might be displayed. The subdued light and the gentle tones of mud walls and aging natural wood create an atmosphere conducive to contemplation. The guests quietly wait for their host to appear. The host opens the sliding door panel, welcomes each guest, returns to the preparation room, and begins serving a small meal.

The meaning of *kaiseki,* the Japanese term for this meal, comes from the name given to a warmed stone that Zen monks used to press against their stomachs to help alleviate the pangs of hunger and cold. It has since come to mean a small meal just sufficient to satisfy hunger.

This meal, the epitome of Japanese cuisine, is the standard against which Japanese food is judged. Meticulous attention is given to every detail of its preparation and service. Ingredients are seasonal, fresh, and simple. There is a selection of foods, some from the ocean and some from the mountains. These are beautifully arranged and served on specially selected plates. The guest not only enjoys the taste of the food, but also appreciates the way it is presented. The food is thus "tasted" in three ways: with eyes, tongue, and heart. The chopsticks used for serving this meal are of freshly cut green bamboo and will not alter the flavor of the food.

After partaking of the meal, the guests watch the host lay fresh charcoal in the fire. Then they are served a moist sweet. They go out into the garden to refresh themselves while the host replaces the scroll with a flower and completes the preparations for serving tea. The host strikes a gong to indicate that the guests may reenter for thick tea.

The mood is quiet, and oneness is felt among the guests, for all will share this one bowl of tea.

Though all utensils have been cleaned in the preparation room, each will be symbolically purified again in the presence of the guests. The willing attitude of the host to serve allows him to harmonize his breathing and movements so that he and his guests may jointly concentrate on this act of making tea. The ceramic tea container and bamboo tea scoop are wiped with a silk cloth. With the bamboo water ladle, hot water is drawn from the kettle and poured into the tea bowl. The bamboo whisk is rinsed and examined carefully. The water is emptied out, and the bowl is wiped with a dampened linen cloth.

Wisps of steam rise from the kettle. The simmering water sounds like the wind as it blows through pines.

The host puts a measured amount of powdered tea into the bowl, adds some hot water, blends the tea with the tea whisk, adds a bit more water, blends it again, and gives it to the first guest.

In the stillness wafts the fragrance of the tea. All the guests share this one bowl of thick dark green tea. Afterward they may request a closer viewing of the tea container, its silk bag, and the tea scoop. Meanwhile, the host removes all other utensils. He reenters the tearoom to answer questions about the utensils the guests have inspected. What is the container's shape? Where was it made? Who carved the tea scoop? Does it have a special name? After this exchange, the host picks up these utensils, leaves the room, and bows to the guests from the door.

Soon the host reenters, carrying the utensils with which to serve thin tea. The mood now is much lighter and the pace quicker. He makes each guest a separate bowl of tea. Light sweets are eaten just before the host whisks the tea. During this time there may be some light conversation, and the guests may request a closer examination of the thin-tea container and tea scoop. They might ask about the lacquer, the shape of the container, and the maker and name of the tea scoop. After this they will quietly once again view flowers and brazier and then leave.

The host opens the guest's entrance and makes a farewell bow to his guests, remaining in the doorway until they are out of sight.

He sits for a moment reflecting on the gathering and then removes all utensils and cleans them, takes down the flower from the alcove, and gives the room a final cleaning. The tearoom is empty. Nothing extraordinary has happened from the perspective of the casual onlooker, but at its best, the experience of both host and guests has been a microcosm of life itself.

"What precisely are the most important things that must be understood and kept in mind at a tea gathering?" A disciple of Sen Rikyu once asked him this question.

His answer was, "Make a delicious bowl of tea; lay the

charcoal so that it heats the water; arrange the flowers as they are in the field; in summer suggest coolness, in winter, warmth; do everything ahead of time; prepare for rain; and give those with whom you find yourself every consideration."

The disciple, somewhat dissatisfied with this answer because he could not find anything in it of such great importance that it could be deemed a secret of the practice, said, "That much I already know. . . ."

Rikyu answered, "Then if you can host a tea gathering without deviating from any of the rules I have just stated, I will become your disciple."

These Seven Rules of Rikyu have been revered and handed down as the most important guides for one's proper attitude in the Way of Tea. Even though we call them rules, they at first seem to be seven totally reasonable and unremarkable things. However, it would be rash to think it unnecessary to take them up for discussion, for they are extremely difficult to observe in our daily life.

The Way of Tea is not merely an art or accomplishment or amusement, but is rather a way of life possessing a strong ethical and moral character. The Seven Rules of Rikyu, defining the attitude of one who practices Tea, are considered a fundamental teaching. As with most truths, the simpler the words, the stronger and more straightforward they are, and the more forcefully they strike our hearts.

I would like to discuss briefly each of the rules, in the hope that they will help you to understand the Way of Tea.

Let us consider the first rule, *"Make a delicious bowl of tea."* The words simply mean that tea should be made so that it is delicious to drink. But what will make it so? There are probably some who think that from a modern standpoint no complicated reasoning is necessary to give the guest a sense of the "good taste" of tea. It is very simple. First, buy the most expensive tea and procure water passed through a filtration system producing a completely tasteless, odorless, and pure liquid; heat it to the one perfect temperature that will bring out the flavor of the tea, whisk the water and tea, and offer it along with the highest-quality sweets. The guest will never fail to find it delicious. In addition, make a great demonstration of your concern for your guest by spending lavishly to appoint the room and landscape the garden; if that is not enough, construct a tearoom of gold and gilt, bargain with dealers of renowned utensils so you can hang a scroll of certified high quality, and use a famous tea bowl handed down through an important family; do not forget to choose all utensils for their utter lack of blemish or flaw; and finally perform the whole ceremony with such obviously high technical skill that the guest will be intimidated into awe-filled silence. If you do all this, some would believe, the guest will undoubtedly believe he has partaken of a delicious bowl of tea.

But I wonder if something of singular importance has not been omitted. Certainly if the host spends money and puts much thought and labor into entertaining his guest, there are some who will return home pleased, with their sense of taste "satisfied." However, this alone is no more than an amusement, a way of enjoying oneself in the company of others. But the Way of Tea is something that teaches, through serving and receiving a bowl of tea, a way of life. Hence, material sufficiency is inadequate. But what then is missing? There is a room to sit in, utensils to serve with, and enough water and tea. What is missing is the sincere heart of the host.

Once a tea grower invited Rikyu to have tea. Overwhelmed with joy at Rikyu's acceptance, the tea grower led him to the tearoom and served tea to Rikyu himself. However, in his excitement his hand trembled and he performed badly, dropping the tea scoop and knocking the tea whisk over. The other guests, disciples of Rikyu, snickered at the tea grower's manner of making tea, but Rikyu was moved to say, "It was the finest."

On the way home, one of the disciples asked Rikyu, "Why were you so impressed by such a shameful performance?" Rikyu answered, "This man did not invite me with the idea of showing off his skill. He simply wanted to serve me tea with his whole heart. He devoted himself completely to making a bowl of tea for me, not worrying about errors. I was struck by that sincerity."

The meaning of the second rule, *"Lay the charcoal so that it heats the water,"* can only be that it is enough to build a charcoal fire so that the water is properly heated. But this procedure must not be regarded as merely placing some pieces of charcoal in a heap and setting them afire. Learning to handle and lay charcoal in the brazier or sunken hearth is just as important as learning the method and manner of preparing tea. The host's level of accomplishment is decided here. A fire arranged properly will burn efficiently and heat the water to the temperature that will best bring out the flavor of the tea. In a deeper sense, this rule directs attention to the lightness of spirit that comes when one sincerely brings all of one's knowledge and technical skill to any task that is for the benefit of one's guest.

All that Tea holds as an ideal of beauty can be said to be fully expressed in *chabana,* flowers for a tea gathering. Precisely where does the beauty lie? What kinds of flowers are used, and how should they be arranged? *"Arrange the flowers as they are in the field,"* the third rule, hints at the answer.

Chabana has no relationship whatsoever to the various schools of flower arrangement; there are no principles of structure or composition. Nor are there rules or restrictions stemming from religious beliefs. However, such flowers as cockscomb and daphne are not generally used for chabana because their strong colors and fragrances are not suited to the tearoom.

Even though the rule states "as they are in the field," this does not mean that the host should take one or two stems and place them in the flower container in imitation of their random blooming in the meadow or on the mountainside. Rather, the host should try to bring to the guest the whole life that lies within each flower: that is, the individual beauty that all flowers possess naturally, the singularly transient life given by nature to the flowers "as they are in the field." This beauty hidden in all flowers can be experienced in one. In other words, rather than looking indiscriminately at an arrangement of many flowers, know the precious life of all flowers represented in a single blossom.

Rikyu was ever aware of this beauty. There is a famous anecdote that illustrates his ability to bring it forth.

One summer, Rikyu cultivated with great devotion a garden full of morning glories. At that time they were a rarity, having been brought to Japan by traders, and people talked of their fresh, unique beauty. This news reached the ear of the military leader Hideyoshi. Wishing to see for himself, Hideyoshi asked Rikyu to hold a tea gathering in the morning so that he could view the flowers; Rikyu immediately began preparations for his visit.

The day of the tea arrived and, looking forward to seeing morning glories blooming in profusion, Hideyoshi set out.

Entering the front gate of Rikyu's house he did not see a single bloom. On the path to the tearoom as well he discovered no flowers, and the cool water in the stone basin reflected nothing but sky and greenery. Dismayed, he entered the tearoom; there, in the subdued light of the papered windows he discerned one perfect morning glory, floating in a container hanging in the tokonoma, indistinct and white, quietly wet with dew.

Historically, chabana has meant one or two flowers or foliage in a simple flower container. This remains unchanged today. The Tea classic *Namboroku* mentions "a single chrysanthemum in a wide-mouthed flower container"; "in a flower basket, white peach blossom"; "in a narrow-mouth [container], one chrysanthemum"; "iris in a length of bamboo." How modest these are!

A flower Rikyu liked to use was the camellia. Because the entire flower drops at once upon withering, to some schools of flower arrangement it has associations with beheading and is therefore considered inappropriate; but for chabana, the camellia's trim beauty is particularly favored. Further, in formal flower arrangement it is considered especially poor form when a flower hangs below the mouth of the flower vase; but in chabana, this is of no concern.

In conclusion, "Arrange the flowers as they are in the field" seems to be telling us to place them naturally, not as they appear in their wild state, but instead enhanced by the skill and heart of the one who seeks beauty through the practice of Tea.

The fourth rule, *"In summer suggest coolness; in winter, warmth,"* appears to be divided into two parts. However, this is a matter of insignificant detail; as far as the basic spirit is concerned, the two are one and the same.

From June through August, a fine way of passing the summer is summed up by practitioners of Tea with the phrase, "the one taste of coolness." This coolness is not produced mechanically by fan or air conditioner. Nor is it some other contrivance to help one endure the heat. Rather, it is a positive way, derived from the physical setting, of enjoying life in the heat of summer.

Imagine how this might be by considering an example. Notice here that there are three areas of concern: the garden path, the tearoom, and the selection of utensils.

You have been invited to a tea gathering in early August. The host has asked you to come at six o'clock in the morning. Proceeding along the path to the tearoom you notice that the host has thoughtfully splashed cooling water on the stepping-stones. The deep green of the shrubbery and moss still seem to hold the cool of the night just ended. The water in the stone basin reminds you of a cool, clear pool. The host has created for you a perfect retreat. You enter the tearoom. It is refreshingly unadorned except for a scroll hanging in the tokonoma. Natural light filters through bamboo shades hanging in front of the windows. Approaching the scroll, you admire the way the poem written on it suggests to you "the one taste of coolness." In the ceramic brazier there is a small, cylindrical iron kettle, dampened as if by dew.

An openwork basket is brought into the room. In it are the utensils used to lay a charcoal fire in the brazier. From the depths of the basket, the host brings out a red lacquer incense container with a carving of an angler on the lid. The still-moist kettle is replaced over the newly laid charcoal.

Next, a light meal is served. Of particular interest is the rice container, a basket lined with glistening green leaves. Then, after serving an ice-cold sweet, the host suggests that you leave the room for a rest and enjoy the shade in the garden while he freshens the room and prepares the utensils for the serving of tea.

Returning to the room, you notice the scroll has been removed; hanging in its place in the tokonoma is a slim basket of woven bamboo holding a white rose of Sharon and a long, thin leaf of summer grass, wet with dew. The water container is of unfinished wood in the shape of a well bucket, its surface thoroughly moistened. The tea scoop has a name suggestive of breezes, rain showers, or other things that bring coolness in summer. The tea bowl for the service of thick tea is light-colored but sturdy.

At a morning gathering, thin tea in a shallow bowl is served immediately after thick tea. The gathering ends near nine o'clock. Thinking back, you remember how unelaborate and modest the utensils were and how the host's attention was given to the selection of each piece to suggest coolness for this morning tea in August.

The phrase ". . . in winter, warmth" is parallel to the suggestion of coolness in summer; their foundations are precisely the same. The arrangement of the garden path, the warmth of the tearoom, the selection of utensils to suggest as well as to actually give warmth, the color of the burning charcoal embers in the sunken hearth, or the lantern's soft reassuring glow—all these are considered carefully to communicate to the guest the blessings of nature and the warmth of the human heart.

"Do everything ahead of time," the fifth rule, means to observe strictly an appointed hour and, preparing ahead of time, to take into consideration the unexpected.

Much is made of punctuality in Japan, in order that public facilities function with greatest efficiency and economy. It is interesting that even during the time of Rikyu this insistence on being punctual was an important admonition. In teaching the proper attitude for Tea, Rikyu emphasized maintaining a certain margin for error in one's preparations for hosting or attending a tea gathering. This allowance for error or the unexpected represents respect for time. At a tea gathering or anywhere else, to squander one's own precious time is bad enough, but to waste the time of another is even worse. In sum, to value one's own time and keep a certain margin is nothing other than to respect the time of others.

The words *"prepare for rain,"* rule six, might bring to mind the image of an English gentleman wearing a derby and a black suit and carrying an umbrella tucked under his arm. In a place like London, one has to worry about the rain constantly. Likewise, when hosting a tea gathering there is no telling what may happen if it rains. One cannot be negligent of such considerations for the guest as umbrellas and special clogs for walking in the wet garden.

With this rule Rikyu further reminds us that we should never be negligent in our preparations and should be able to calmly adapt to circumstances. The chief aim of the teacher of Tea is to nurture in the student the ability to respond with composure to any occasion, whatever may happen, with an open heart and a free and direct mind.

There is a saying, "If there is preparation, there will be no regret." While the apparent meaning of "prepare for rain" is simply that we should be prepared in all practical details, beyond this it implies that the attitude of the heart is important. It is the free and magnanimous heart that counts. If you fully endeavor in your practice, it is not so difficult to gain the necessary self-confidence, and whatever the occasion, you will carry on with spontaneity.

Once Rikyu hosted a tea gathering to which he invited a merchant. While the gathering was in progress, a powerful lord visited Rikyu on business and, upon learning of the gathering, requested that he be admitted as a guest. Rikyu answered that the merchant was the principal guest, but if the lord found a lower position in the room acceptable, he was welcome to join. The lord had no objection to such an arrangement; without the least ill-feeling, he took the last place and the tea gathering continued congenially. As stated in the *Namboroku*:

> The tea manner of the thatched hut follows the spirit of the master [Rikyu]; the equality of noble and humble, put into practice as the fundamental meaning of the path that leads to the tearoom, surpasses the rules of the temples, and is worthy of reverence.

One feels high regard here for the dauntlessness of Rikyu, who refused to flatter the powerful and, observing the spirit and rules of Tea, put a great lord in the last seat because there already was a principal guest, although that guest was but a merchant. At the same time, one cannot suppress admiration for the lord, who willingly accepted the last position and enjoyed the tea.

In this story we can see two aspects of the spirit of Tea. One is that quality in which, however distinguished or humble people may be, as human beings they are equals. Social standards of high and low, rich and poor, have no place in the tearoom. The other aspect is the seventh rule, *"Give those with whom you find yourself every consideration."* Neither host nor guest acts merely as he pleases, but both act with mutual consideration; both take pleasure in their shared moment in the tearoom.

The essential requirement of any tea gathering is that there be host and guest. Their relationship is of singular importance. For this reason, one must give great attention to making it harmonious.

Examining the ideographs making up the Japanese word for human being, *ningen*, we can understand the meaning of human being in terms of the space or interval between one person and another. The first character, person *(nin)*, and the second one, interval or space *(gen)*, suggest that one becomes truly human through interaction with another.

Whether as host or as guest at a tea gathering, one must remember that there is neither audience nor performer, but a true interaction of human beings. Through sympathetic co-ordination, host and guest become one.

It is often said that the ideal to strive for at a tea gathering is represented by the Zen expression *muhinshu*. *Mu* refers to nothingness; *hin*, to the guest or to the one who is trained in in the principles of Zen; and *shu*, to the host. Of course it does not refer to any literal nonexistence of host and guest, but to the absence of differentiation between them. When host and guest are in harmony at a tea gathering, they merge into a single entity that transcends their respective roles.

Of great importance to the Way of Tea is the concept of *kokoro ire*. Written with two characters, the first represents "heart-spirit-mind"; the second, "to put in." In other words, the host puts his whole being into the preparation for a tea gathering and executes his role with the intent of creating an atmosphere wherein the guest can find tranquility. The guest enters the tearoom with the intent of giving his host all of his heart, spirit, and mind, through his open acceptance of all that the host is doing for him. This is not a question of technique alone, but of honest thankfulness.

In Tea the expression *ichigo ichie* is frequently heard. It means "one time, one meeting." Each tea gathering is an opportunity for an experience that will never occur again in one's life.

When the Zen priest Kokei, who had long been a friend of Rikyu, was sent into exile by Hideyoshi, Rikyu held a farewell tea for him. On this special occasion, Rikyu hung a scroll of the calligraphy of a Zen master; this scroll was one of Hideyoshi's most precious tea utensils and had been given to Rikyu for repair of its mounting. If Hideyoshi had known that Rikyu had dared to hang this scroll, particularly on such an occasion for a man he had just ordered into exile, it probably would have cost Rikyu his life. As this was to be the final parting with his friend Kokei, the spirit of ichigo ichie was fully manifested in Rikyu's choice of this scroll.

Where else in the world can you find just one bowl of tea so politely offered? A guest says to the one sitting next to him, "Excuse me while I go first." The second guest replies, "After you." The first guest accepts and says to the host, "I will drink the tea." He does not assume that he naturally takes the first bowl of tea because he is seated at the head. When he finishes his bowl of tea, the next person sometimes suggests that he have another. The first guest does not accept immediately, but says instead, "I have had a bowl already; please have some." This etiquette forms the basis for a thoughtful relationship that means: I am not satisfied if I alone drink; let us drink in turn. This spirit of concern for others first is a very important element and can be practiced in our daily life.

It is often asked why the host does not join the guests. It

seems odd to see guests entertaining each other while the host withdraws. There are, of course, special cases when the host joins the guests at their suggestion, but most often he declines, in order to concentrate his entire spirit and body on serving. This painstaking attention that is required of the host is not felt as a burden, but as a delicate communication.

SETTING THE STAGE

THE HISTORY OF THE WAY OF TEA can be viewed almost as a history of Japanese taste. During the fifteenth century in the gardens of the Gold and Silver pavilions of Kyoto, guests would enjoy a leisurely walk along a garden path circling an artificial lake, resting here and there to admire the ingenious renderings in miniature of famous views. They would then enter a spacious room to view grand displays of Chinese scrolls and ceramic wares. Proceeding further, a second room set with a sumptuous feast would greet them, and after having sampled the delicacies they would then drink tea. In that era, only things of Chinese origin were valued; this was seen in the usage of Chinese utensils for the service of tea.

Murata Shuko opposed this tendency. He taught that the practice of Tea should serve to provide calm, rather than be the setting for such display. Part of his legacy to his disciples, and later to all Japanese, was a taste for utensils of Japanese as well as Chinese origin. Shuko said he preferred the moon partially shrouded by clouds. He was profoundly moved, not by the bright moon in a clear sky, but by the moon as it appeared behind clouds. In the same spirit he preferred the muted beauty of simple, imperfect objects. The search for beauty in such objects led him to say that "the most important thing is to seek as many admirable traits in Japanese objects as in Chinese." He was followed in these teachings by Takeno Jo-o, who further simplified the procedures for making tea and sought to bring it into even more humble circumstances.

Finally it was Sen Rikyu who brought together the teachings of the past and instilled a greater simplicity within the context of the discipline. Seeking to harmonize the many elements common to Tea and ordinary life, he had a distinct preference for native wares and Korean wares. These were generally less refined than those of Chinese origin. His encouragement of the use of ordinary wares extended to domestic kilns, and today he is considered responsible in great part for the development of Japanese ceramic art.

Let us turn our imagination to Rikyu's era. It is not difficult to picture the world of tea in chaos, with tea connoisseurs competing with one another and using tea gatherings as a forum for such things as politics and religious controversy.

Acting in these conditions, Rikyu gave form to Tea with this enlightened teaching:

> Tea is nought but this:
> First you heat the water,
> Then you make the tea.
> Then you drink it properly.
> That is all you need to know.

This insight of Rikyu's was an admonition to the Tea world of his day, and these ideas have come down to us as a fundamental philosophy. However, if the ultimate form of Tea can be reduced to the bare simplicity of Rikyu's poem, we may wonder why so much fuss could be created out of something so apparently simple. The difficulty lies rather in the path to the attainment of simplicity, and there is no way to arrive at this point quickly.

Leading to the tearoom is a garden path called a *roji*. The literal meaning of roji is "dewy ground." In Buddhism, this world in which we live is called "the fiery house of three worlds." We pass through the "dewy ground" leaving "the fiery house" and live for a moment in a place of purity and revelation. To walk along this garden path is to discard worldly title, position, and means.

Walking through the garden, the atmosphere of which is reminiscent of mountains or deep valleys, you come to the tea hut. You enter through a very low, small doorway. Its size and location in the hut require you to crawl through rather than stride through. Four hundred years ago when social classes were clearly differentiated and samurai wore swords, no one could enter the tea hut armed or, for that matter, carrying any belongings except those that were necessary for the gathering. There was a rack attached to the outside wall of the tea hut near the entrance where a samurai could leave his weapons. Because the entrance is very low, even the smallest person has to bend down and in so doing look at his feet. This is a significant gesture for a human being, because entering in such a way with the head lowered is a humbling experience and will bring about a certain change in attitude.

The tearoom is a vacant space with no ornamentation, empty of everything but its own architectural elements. Therefore, when inviting guests the host has to, in a sense, "set the stage." There are certain standards for this, but these can be modified in many ways according to the host's feelings at the time, as well as to his experience and talents. The room may be arranged simply, in muted tones, like the black and white of an ink painting, or it may be colorful. It is almost as though the host had to be an interior decorator. This, of course, requires a certain skill, but more important is the art of combining the different elements; careful attention is essential in assembling different utensils of clay, metal, wood, lacquer, and other materials, in an elegant but reserved manner. This combination is part of a tea gathering.

A scroll is hung in the alcove of the tearoom and must be selected with special care. It is one of the most direct means for the host to express the theme for a particular tea gathering. Often the scroll is one written by a Zen master. A scroll may be a painting, or it may be rendering of a classic phrase of Zen wisdom, a poem, or any appropriate words.

When hanging it, one cannot simply assume that it is well chosen if it suits the alcove and spatial character of the tearoom. Apart from its artistic merit, size, shape, tone, or other properties, one must consider the season in selecting a scroll. In the Way of Tea, the season is of great significance. It has been said, "Spring has flowers, summer has cool breezes, fall has the moon, winter has snow." To best appreciate the season, the host hangs an appropriate scroll. In fall, a fall theme is best; in winter, a winter theme. This kind of small thoughtfulness is essential.

Scrolls have many meanings. They may be seasonal or inspirational. When the guests view the scroll they may be touched by its message or taste the flavor of a season.

The *Namboroku* states that "the meaning of the calligraphy on the scroll is in the spirit of both the person who composed the words and the person who wrote them." Thus, knowledge of the life and thought of the person who wrote the scroll, as well as the actual meaning of the words or painting, all come to bear on the guest's understanding of the theme of a tea gathering.

Flowers are also placed in the alcove. The flowers must be carefully chosen—simple and unpretentious flowers of the season. Contrary to most ideas of flower arrangement, by which flowers are arranged "artistically," for Tea one places flowers as they would be found in nature. Rikyu taught that flowers for Tea should be "as they are in the field." However, nothing is so difficult as trying to arrange them in such a manner. This can only be done with a mind in tune with nature. Thus the scroll and the flowers in their container have to be arranged with contrast and comparison in mind, in keeping with the space of the tearoom and the alcove wall, and the theme of the tea gathering.

Rikyu believed that the tearoom itself should feature nothing to distract the mind and that it was the place in which utensils of varying color, size, and shape, as well as distinctions among the guests, were brought together and exercised their roles, melding to create harmony. This still holds true today. In Tea one must be ever attentive to the details of selection to create and achieve this harmony.

The appropriate combination of the various utensils reveals the heart or sincerity of the host. Thus, how the utensils are used and their various qualities are matters of serious concern.

To prepare tea, several utensils are necessary, such as a container for the powdered green tea leaves, a scoop to measure out this tea, a tea whisk, and a bowl in which the powdered tea and hot water are whipped and from which the tea is sipped. These items are not thought of as mere utilitarian pieces, not valued simply as antiquated art objects; they are "like a mirror upon which the host's mind is reflected." In orderly procedure they are brought into the room where the guests are seated. Tea is prepared and offered, and when the gathering is over the utensils are returned to their proper places, again in an orderly procedure.

The high quality of the craftsmanship and design of tea utensils is evident at first glance. They have an uncommonly good sense about them. The slight curve of the tea scoop, the fall of the glaze on a tea bowl, the black crispness of the lacquer tea container, and the slightly curled tines of the tea whisk are not merely decorative elements, but are necessary details that will contribute to the overall atmosphere of a tea gathering. Whether they are seen in an exhibition case or held in the hands, there is a certain quality about the utensils used in the preparation of tea that speaks to anyone. In the setting of the tea gathering they are given life and are able to suggest a world of the spirit beyond time or place.

Occasionally a tea gathering is held with an astounding selection of utensils. However, should the host and guests concern themselves with the utensils alone, to the detriment of their unique personal relationship, the gathering will have the taint of a private showing in an art gallery. Such gatherings based solely on display are worthless as far as the spirit of Tea is concerned. Only when the relationship of the host and guest is placed first do mute utensils come to life and show their worth.

Gengensai (1810–77), the eleventh-generation Grand Tea Master of Urasenke, was a man of vision. His was a difficult age of change that saw the abolition of the feudal clans and the beginnings of the modern nation of Japan during the 1860s. A man of his times, he adopted Western ideas into the practice of Tea. In 1872, at an international exhibition in Kyoto, he prepared and served tea sitting on a stool at a table. Guests, too, were seated on stools at tables. The more tradition-oriented among the Japanese were critical. Even so, risking his reputation, he boldly implemented the new style, and it has continued into the present.

What is important to learn from his innovation is that it was made out of consideration for his guests. People from all parts of the globe were to visit Kyoto for the exhibition. He desired to serve them tea. Knowing that they did not sit on tatami, he designed tables and stools and perfected a new procedure for serving tea.

In keeping with this idea, I always encourage those who are living abroad to search for and use whatever utensils can be found at hand, whether or not they are intended for tea. However, when making substitutions or changes, it is absolutely essential that the fundamental relationship of host and guest remain foremost in one's mind. Substitution for substitution's sake is without meaning. Follow the example of Gengensai and, with the mind of a guest, anticipate the needs of your guests.

Rikyu fixed the standards for serving and drinking a bowl of tea. These may seem at first troublesome, but without them people would be unsure as to the most efficient movements of the body, as well as the practical procedures involved in making a charcoal fire, cleaning the tearoom, and so on. Although the manner and order are all fixed, when different people prepare and serve tea, they are able to give life to the standards with their own character and heart.

The Way of Tea has undergone many generations of nurturing and refinement. Each one of the procedures for making tea has been polished so that it is difficult to perform it any other way with greater skill or ease. Thus, the first step in the practice of Tea is to learn each movement faithfully. Gradually, you will show more and more the result of your study of the order and manner of preparing tea.

Once these skills are learned and assimilated, you can then go beyond them. But at first you must learn the steps, paying careful attention to each detail. Gradually, after many repetitions, it is almost as if the procedure performs itself. It becomes part of your body, as natural as walking.

Once you have learned how to sit and how to serve tea according to the rules of the discipline of Tea, you are free to use your mind and body at will. When you know how to use this freedom, you can at last serve tea in a serious manner to your guests.

It would be easy to assume that you must steel yourself for the task of hosting or attending a tea gathering. There is a danger, however, in trying too hard; Rikyu warns against this in a passage in the *Namboroku*:

> It is good for the host and guest to try their best, and in consequence satisfy each other. However, it is not good for them to aim for the goal of satisfaction from the beginning.

It seems wise therefore to abandon any goal of achieving success. Giving up this goal may in itself result in a successful experience.

There is every possibility that at some point you will blunder and place a utensil in the wrong place or make some other mistake. It is then that your long training will make itself apparent if you can resolve the problem with composure. Of course, being able to make tea without error is also the achievement of long practice. But the matter of greatest importance is to be able to manage quickly and smoothly if any failing or mishap occurs.

When I am asked to take brush and put to paper a phrase or a poem, the important point is not the quality or proficiency of my calligraphy, but that it conveys the timeless verity of the words. Therefore, as anyone does when he enters a tearoom, I bow before the alcove where the scroll is hanging, even if it is my own calligraphy. More than just a formal gesture, this is a bow of humility before the words that are written.

Some people think it strange for me to bow before one of my own works. They think, too, that a potter having tea from a bowl of his own making and bowing in appreciation is strange. They forget the humility with which one holds a tea bowl in both hands, bowing not to the bowl alone but also out of respect and thankfulness for one's relatedness to all that went into the making of the bowl and the tea within: the earth, the clay, the potter's talents, the sun, the tea plants. One is also expressing gratitude for having been given the opportunity to be there at that one moment to receive the tea. This thankfulness is then made manifest in a small act of humility that is in the same spirit as bending low to enter the small doorway of the tea hut. After raising the bowl and bowing slightly, the guest turns the bowl halfway around so that he does not drink from the front, or "face," of it, but from the back. Together, these acts of thankfulness and humility are an important part of the experience of Tea.

In response to a young man's questions about morning worship, the Buddha taught:

When you bow to the east give thanks for your parents. When you bow to the south, give thanks for your teachers. When you bow to the west give thanks for your wife and children. When you bow to the north give thanks for your friends, acquaintances, and all the world's people. Looking skyward, be thankful for your presence in the universe, and looking down to the earth be thankful for its bounty.

Prior to making thick tea we specially prepare ourselves and purify our minds and the utensils to be used. One step in this preparation is the careful examination of the four edges of a silk wiping cloth. This process also represents an offering of thanks through the four cardinal points, each point represented by one of the four edges, comparable to the sutra quoted above. We are not just purifying the utensils and our minds, but, as the sutra implies, realizing humbly our relationship with all that is around us, with the universe. Without this, the serving of tea becomes a perfunctory and empty form. This pure, simple, and thankful heart that gives meaning to the forms of Tea comes with a pursuit of self-training and discipline that is akin to the practice of Zen.

THE PLACE OF PRACTICE

IN THE TIME OF BUDDHA, a man was walking deep in the mountains in search of a place where he could discipline himself to understand his spirit. While searching he chanced to meet one of Buddha's disciples.

"Sir, from where do you come?" he asked. The disciple answered directly, "I've come from my place of practice." Thinking that this man knew of the very place for which he had been searching, he asked the disciple, "Sir, I am looking for that same place. Please take me there." The disciple answered, "The place of practice lies in the pure and honest spirit where there is no false vanity." Startled, the man saw that a place of practice and discipline is not only seen with the eyes. The place of practice is the spirit. The spirit searches to enlighten itself. It does not matter whether it is a room where one practices tea or meditates; any place that is peaceful is the place where you can find your own spirit.

The poet Hakurakuten was given an official assignment in the country. Knowing that from then on he would have to take responsibility for governing many people, he, too, sought out a famous Zen priest for advice.

The priest whom Hakurakuten approached had no temple. Instead he would always sit in meditation at the top of a tree, looking like a big black bird.

At the foot of the tree, Hakurakuten asked what the ideal spirit is and what he should do to be a good governor. The priest did not move. Hakurakuten looked up at him from below and shouted, "If you doze off, sitting up there, you'll fall and hurt yourself."

Hearing this, the priest yelled back, "What are you saying! Your feet aren't even touching the ground, are they?" Hakurakuten was so surprised by the priest's words that he looked afresh at his own feet and realized that they were not on the ground at all. With that, bowing at the foot of the tree, he begged the priest to teach him.

The priest responded, "That's easy enough. The leader does good for the people; he does not commit any evil acts; he purifies his own mind. This is Buddha's doctrine." He then added that if only these things were done, Hakurakuten would govern his country well.

But Hakurakuten, harboring a doubt, said that anyone was capable of such things. The priest's reply was, "If that is so then I will become your disciple and you my master."

There is a story about two friends. Both of them had been good students, but one received an inheritance from his parents, worked skillfully and persistently, and was rewarded in his efforts by attaining a respectable social position. The other man, who had studied just as well, only dreamed of getting rich quickly and, unlike his friend, wandered about rather than working hard.

One day, after a long separation, the wandering man was invited to visit his successful friend, who wanted somehow to help him. After all, the wanderer basically had a good character, and it was not right that he should drift about aimlessly. Unfortunately, on the very day he had invited the poor man, some urgent business arose and it became unavoidable that he be away from home for a short time, but, after having extended an invitation, he could not abruptly break his promise. When the poor man arrived he was served food and drink and soon fell asleep. The successful man, who had money and social status, wanted to do something for his poor friend who had neither. But to give something material or to openly do him a special favor would be distasteful for both men. So while his friend slept, the wealthy man stitched a jewel into his sleeve, thinking that someday he would discover it and realize what had happened. Then he slipped out to take care of his business.

When the poor man woke up, the master of the house was gone; he became angry at such a lack of courtesy, and though a member of the family tried to explain, the man was too furious to listen and he left the house grumbling. Needless to say, he was unaware of the treasure that was in his sleeve.

After several years had passed, the two of them happened to meet. While the one had become even more successful and developed a wider reputation, the other man, beaten by his own feelings of inferiority, had become cynical. He was still unaware of the jewel that had been sewn into his sleeve. Without knowing of his friend's goodwill, he had lost all self-confidence and continued to lead the life of a vagabond.

That day, upon meeting his successful friend, the poor man bitterly rebuked him for his rudeness at their last meeting. At last the man of wealth said to him, "I cannot remember anything to give you reason to rebuke me. You got drunk and fell asleep. I had to leave and I stitched a jewel into a fold of your sleeve, praying that it would give you the capital from which you might somehow make a living."

Astonished, the poor man looked in his sleeve and sure enough there was the jewel, sewn in as his friend had said. Only that part of his ragged, torn clothes, had remained intact. That treasure received from his friend became his salvation. From then on, he prayed every night and day and worked diligently. After two or three years he gained great wealth and came to be a respected man of good character.

Though this may seem to be a simple story, it in fact comes from a famous Zen text. The jewel refers to the Buddha-nature within each of us. Although everyone possesses this treasure, most people are unaware of it. The man of standing who helped his friend to gain awareness represents the Buddha. The friend who lacked awareness of his friend's goodwill represents humanity. Not knowing of that treasure we all possess, our abilities are lost and we idle through a meaningless life.

In one Tea teacher's house hangs a scroll that says:

The Place of Self Humiliation.

When you enter the Way of Tea, no matter how you think you may disgrace yourself, it will not be taken as disgrace or shame. Make mistakes, be rebuked, stand corrected, and learn. Rikyu wrote a poem with a similar meaning as a guide for the student of Tea:

> Fight your shame.
> Throw out your pride and learn all you can
>   from others.
> This is the basis of a successful life.

The Way is wherever people discipline themselves through training. It is not to be found in books. It is through direct experience with our own bodies and not only our intellects that we can attain this state.

When people set out to learn something they become obsessed with the process and lose heart when it seems they cannot master it. Thinking themselves stupid and believing that others probably think so too, they forget what they were trying so hard to learn. Many people learning Tea, having heard that it is complicated, try to memorize the steps for making tea and become perplexed and disillusioned if it is difficult to remember the order. There is a lesson in the following story that should help us have patience.

In the time of Buddha lived two brothers. The elder, named Maha, was famed for his good memory and was regarded as a great man, but Sri, the younger, could not remember a thing, and it was said that he would never amount to anything. Even though Maha tried to teach him, Sri was never able to remember what he had been taught. Finally Maha gave up and threw his brother out of the house, telling him to get an education somewhere else. Later, a tearful Sri happened to meet the Buddha and was soon pouring out his story. Listening to him, the Buddha thought that here was a man who could learn something, so he handed Sri a broom and a dustbin, telling him, "Cleanse your heart, remove all the dust of the world. Every day sweep and clean." However, this was easier said than done, for when he began to sweep he forgot the admonition, and once he remembered the Buddha's words he forgot what he had been told to do. However, after many years of cleaning, sweeping, and chanting "Cleanse away the dust," he finally rid his own heart of the dust of the world, reached enlightenment, and became a man of position.

The student of Tea once on the path must put away his doubts about himself and ignore the slighting remarks of others. He must give the greatest attention to his study and practice. Tea, like cleaning, is not a skill to memorize but one that is acquired slowly by the body and the spirit.

Silently purify yourself as you go through the procedures of making tea. Listen and acquire a sensitivity to the sound of water poured from a bamboo water ladle into a tea bowl or kettle. In this pure sound is the realm of nonattachment. To enter this realm is one reason why we practice over and over again the same procedures in making tea. My father believed and practiced this constantly. Making and drinking a bowl of tea involves no right and no wrong. It is a simple, open, and honest meeting of minds, beyond wisdom, experience, and point of view.

THE NEED FOR A DISCIPLINE

ALL OF MAN'S ACTIONS originate in his self-consciousness. We tend to think that our subjective reality is only a fraction of a far greater objective reality. Conversely, the Chinese Zen monk Rinzai admonishes that external reality is but one aspect of subjective reality and that we must be neither oppressed not unsettled by the objective world but must set ourselves free from it. We must not rely upon the world of objects for guidance or knowledge. We have been seduced into weighing the advantages and disadvantages of every action, leaning this way, then that, thus forgetting our own real center. Talking, we utter absurdities and end up speaking at cross-purposes. Confronted by all sorts of problems, we tend to deal with them superficially, not understanding their true meaning. Vacillating between action and inaction until the next problem arises, we end up going along with the current of the times, muttering with the crowd, "After all, what can be done about it anyway?"

Confusing appearances with reality and worrying about what is in our path, we forget to prepare ourselves for our destiny, and we lose our way, our humanity, and our heart in the process. In our everyday life we are buffeted by forces beyond our control. We are controlled by objects; the user becomes the used.

The Rinzai sect of Zen says that we should be centered so that wherever we are, whatever happens, we never lose the infantlike primal mind we are born with. This primal mind is the same as the no-mind or emptiness of mind of Zen. If we are one with it we can overcome our self-consciousness and attachments. In order for us to reach this state we need a discipline or way along which to travel in search of our primal mind. Similar to the way given by a koan, it must be directly applicable to our lives.

A verse written by a T'ang-dynasty Chinese priest describes this state of mind. A prose rendition might read:

There is a man who is so poor that he eats wood and wears clothes made of grass. But his heart is clear like the moon and his mind is calm and nothing disturbs him. If someone asks him, "Where do you live?" he replies, "In the green mountains by the pure water."

The man's answer is a poetic device that can also mean "in all of nature" or, by extension, "all over the world." Though at first this poem may seem insignificant, it is an expression of a centered state of mind that perceives the grandness of nature and, at the same time, feels unity with it. How great it would be when asked, "Where do you live?" to be able to reply, "All over the world."

THE TASTE OF TEA AND ZEN

THE TEA MASTER SEN SOTAN (1578–1658), grandson of Rikyu, said that the taste of Tea and Zen are one and the same. He also said, "The Way of Tea cannot be codified nor can it be condensed into rules to be followed. It is enough if you can glean something that is of use from my everyday musings about Tea." These words are equally applicable to Zen.

We might also say that everything applicable to the Way of Zen is applicable to a tea gathering. In the words of Sen Rikyu:

Remember that fine houses and rare food are mere panaceas of this mundane world, for shelter is enough if it protects from the rain, and food is sufficient if it satisfies hunger. These are the teachings of the Buddha and the Way of Tea. With your own hands bring wood and water, heat the water and make tea. Offer it to the Buddha, to others, and then partake of it yourself. Arrange flowers and burn incense. These actions are taken together for the purpose of following the example of the Buddha.

61

In offering a bowl of tea to Buddha and then presenting it to our guests and finally drinking it ourselves, Tea and Zen become one, helping us to enrich our lives and to feel gratitude and respect for others.

A religious practice, whether Buddhist or not, is important in Tea. This does not mean that you should endeavor to be a saint, but rather that you should always try to use your knowledge and wisdom to cultivate yourself.

Though the word Zen comes from the Sanskrit word *dhyana,* which means meditation, Zen itself is not meditation. Zen is practice, a strict self-training. In the Way of Tea, if we do not have the attitude that daily life itself is the discipline of Zen, then the act of preparing a bowl of tea becomes only one of form, a mere posturing.

The philosophy of the Way of Tea descends from Zen and the practice itself was largely inspired by the austerities of Zen monks, such as Ikkyu and Murata Shuko; Takeno Jo-o was a devotee of Zen, and his disciple and successor, Sen Rikyu, lived according to the principles of Zen outside of the temple.

In the early days of the Kamakura period (1185–1392) when Zen Buddhism was just beginning to spread in Japan, the priest Eisai (1141–1215) returned to Kyoto from study in China, bringing with him some tea seeds. The plants that grew from these seeds thrived in the hills surrounding Kyoto. In his book on the subject of tea, Eisai noted the efficacy of tea in regulating the body, especially the heart, and explained its power to stabilize blood pressure. He also explained how tea drinking contributes to one's peace of mind. Eisai's book and some powdered tea were presented as gifts to Shogun Minamoto Sanetomo (1191–1219), who was encouraged to drink tea also as a remedy when suffering from a hangover.

62

Tea as drunk in temples in China came into wide usage among Zen monks in Japan who drank it for endurance in their training, refreshment in their rituals, and even as a means of promoting Zen in society. This last aspect of its usage, however, differentiated it from its Chinese origins. It did not remain the drink of only the educated and higher classes; by the Muromachi period (1392–1573) it was a refreshment enjoyed by members of all classes.

Two important conditions fostered the birth of the discipline of the Way of Tea. First, during the Muromachi period people sought enlightenment through the Zen methods of self-development and intuitive personal discovery, and the practice of drinking tea was part of the life style of Zen monks. Second, a century of civil wars and uprisings had left Japanese society in a shambles; people sought something to help them endure the hardships and privations of the time. In response to these desires, the practice of drinking tea flourished, especially among the nobles.

From the middle of the sixteenth century, a movement away from the style of Tea practiced among the aristocracy developed in Kyoto. Led by members of the merchant class, it rejected the connoisseurship of tea-utensil experts and the preeminent position held by their prized articles from China. Practitioners of the new style of Tea removed the tea gathering from the luxurious reception rooms of the nobility and created a suitable space in Buddhist temples by partitioning off large halls with folding screens. They abandoned Chinese wares and selected instead Japanese articles, many of folk origin, as well as utensils with imperfections. The new movement brought a lively, creative age into being. Within this milieu it was Rikyu, an ardent follower of Zen, who eventually succeeded in unifying its various components into the form of Tea that still exists today. Rikyu describes the practice and training of Tea in the *Namboroku* in terms applicable to the tearoom or the temple:

> There are many ways to put into practice in our own lives the teachings of the great masters of the past. In Zen, truth is pursued through the discipline of meditation in order to realize enlightenment, while in Tea we use training in the actual procedures of making tea to achieve the same end.

In one school of Zen Buddhism, a disciple is given a problem or question called a koan. It is not a question to interpret and solve with the intellect. The disciple has to project himself into the problem, so that eventually his heart becomes one with it. At that instant he reaches enlightenment (satori). The character representing satori is made of two parts: "heart" and "self." Enlightenment, then, is reached when the disciple knows his own heart.

I would like to give an example in order to show how difficult answering a koan can be, though the story may at first sound ludicrous. This is a very famous koan about an old woman and a priest. An old woman who wanted to take care of a priest had a hut built in which he could live. He disciplined himself rigorously to become a high priest, while the old woman looked after his daily needs. Months, years elapsed, and the time came for her to test the priest. She asked the aid of a young woman who was her neighbor: "I want you to serve the priest his food today. He is meditating sitting facing the wall. When you take his food there, he will eat it, give his thanks and then continue his sitting. I beg you to do me a favor then. When you withdraw the tray, without a word, embrace him and carefully observe his response." The woman, though reluctant, carried in the tray as the old woman had told her to do. The priest accepted the meal and thanked her, looking as serious as usual, and finished the meal, expressing his thanks. The woman removed the tray and, as instructed, advanced to embrace him. He pushed her away, and said, "Since the old tree is on the cold rock, there is no heat for the three winters." The old woman, upon hearing his response, angrily kicked him out, telling him to begin his discipline again, and burned down the hut.

Imagine an old withered tree standing on a cold rock. In Zen, "three winters" means the three coldest months of winter. Thus, what the priest meant was that, even though the woman might come to him, he was as an old tree clinging to a rock in the dead of winter; he did not have the spark of life.

Similar encounters sometimes occur in your life. How do you react? If, like the priest, you were suddenly embraced by circumstance, how would you behave? Such a situation often exposes one's way of life. If merely bound by forms, you might refuse, as the priest did. It would be no waste of time to assign yourself this question as a koan.

FURYU

HISTORICALLY, RATHER THAN SPECULATING about life, the Japanese have assimilated certain concepts, directly applying them to both the material and spiritual aspects of life.

One such concept is *furyu*. Looking at the characters that make up this word, we find that *fu* means wind and *ryu* means to flow. This suggests that our spirit should flow through life like the wind that flows through all of nature. Identifying with nature in this manner necessarily creates a state of mind with a detached, objective quality. We are not emotionally swept away by the marvels of nature; we appreciate them within the natural course of existence. Furyu, not confined to any particular social class, was evident in the lives of nobles, samurai, and ordinary people who, desiring peace in life, naturally loved flowers and birds, admired the moon, and often captured these moments in their verse. The well-known haiku by Basho illustrates this perfectly.

> Old pond,
> A frog jumps in,
> The sound of water.

This is a deceptively simple poem, and one might suppose it easy to compose a similar one. However, it is soon apparent in trying to do so that the feeling of nature is not easily or precisely evoked if one is lacking furyu. Furyu points out only what is absolutely essential for balance and proportion. On the other hand, furyu refuses to be perfect; it includes the imperfect. With mountains, streams, flowers, and the passing of the seasons kept in mind, with the spirit of furyu, we make a bowl of tea.

Furyu as a philosophy of life is certainly not only the possession of writers or artists. Rikyu often taught how furyu could be found in simple acts of anyone's daily life.

Once, at the home of an American acquaintance, I found hanging in an open window a pair of metal chopsticks, the kind used for arranging a charcoal fire. When I asked my friend why they were there, I was told, "When the wind blows they strike each other and make the most beautiful sound." I was delightfully amazed; they were his wind bell. A Japanese would never use them in any way other than to handle charcoal, but here they were serving a completely different purpose. This insight was so perfectly furyu that I almost did not take notice of it, and with that realization I experienced a twofold surprise.

It is impossible not to be impressed from time to time by the exquisite balance and harmony of nature; it is filled with a dignity and purpose beyond human achievement. We can sense a kind of stability among the elements even while experiencing an ever-changing creation in the cycle of seasons.

Dramatic upheavals of the natural order do occur, of course, but storm and earthquake seem only a temporary imbalance, like the ripples caused by a pebble thrown into water. The serene balance again returns. Four seasons have come in turn for countless ages beyond man's reckoning.

We, too, are a product of nature. Therefore we should not busy ourselves trying to conquer and exploit it. The feeling of accord between nature and human beings has long been a part of the Japanese relationship with nature. For example, while the oppression of summer heat seems difficult to overcome, this season is indispensible for the balance and harmony of nature. Reflecting a desire to adapt to, rather than avoid or challenge, the heat in Japan, many contrivances lessen the discomfort of this time: summer confections and the sound of wind bells suggest the feeling of coolness, while houses have traditionally been built for coolness in summer. An important lesson for all of us, then, is to learn to live in accord with nature, meeting with a positive attitude even those aspects with which we feel discomfort. According to an exchange in a collection of Zen koans:

Q: What can be done about the extremes of weather, the hot and cold?

A: If you're so concerned about it why don't you go somewhere where there are no variations in the temperature?

With spring come the flowers, with summer the cool breezes, with autumn the crystal clarity of the moon, and with winter the snow. This eternal procession is a wonderful thing, but how sad that so few of us can appreciate each season. In winter's cold we long for summer, while in summer's heat we wish for autumn breezes.

In Zen, when you become one with the cold or heat, the extremes of hot and cold disappear. This realization of nonduality applies to all the dualisms that plague man: vanity and envy, happiness and sorrow, life and death, wealth and poverty, love and hatred—these can all be integrated. The lifework of becoming one with the smallest daily task leads to the union of the mind with the seasons and with nature. Only then can we appreciate that whatever season we are now experiencing, it is the best.

One of Rikyu's seven rules is "in summer suggest coolness, in winter, warmth." Of course we all seek coolness in the heat of the summer, but there is more than one way to obtain it. One is the short-lived coolness of air conditioning; then there is the longer-lasting coolness that comes from adjusting one's state of mind to take advantage of whatever coolness nature provides. The practice of Tea leads us to appreciate this second coolness. However, many people today may find it difficult to understand this, having lost the will and ability to control their craving for material comfort. Trying to modify civilization for the better, industrial development is quickly separating man from nature. Accustomed to doing whatever we want easily and quickly, we find ourselves increasingly alienated from nature. Prior to the industrial revolution in Japan, the Japanese lived in harmony with nature and developed the custom of becoming one with it, and one with each other, through sharing a bowl of tea. We can learn much from their experience.

The harmony and balance between man and nature can be seen in terms of the material and spiritual in human life. Material culture has flourished because of technological development and will no doubt continue to fulfill many of our aspirations in the future. The extreme development of the material side of our lives, however, does not seem to have brought us happiness and satisfaction. Our zeal for material prosperity may have at the same time destroyed our spiritual welfare, our harmony and serenity, in the same way that great technological advancements have been made at the expense of natural resources.

Scientific and mechanical technology has brought about affluence that could not have been imagined by our grandfathers. Wherever you look in the world, beyond the obvious differences between the economically advanced and the developing nations, the omnipotence of technology, the priority of economics, and the supremacy of growth seem to be advancing apace in every country. In our efforts to challenge and subdue nature, we must still continue to live in harmony with it, though these two attitudes may seem contradictory. To put it another way, the spiritual must coexist with the material.

After an absence of some twenty years, an American friend of mine returned to Japan. Since he had been here with the Occupation forces he was amazed at the incredible changes that had taken place. Previously each locality had had its own individual flavor; one could feel the essence of a place. However, the combination of industrial innovation and the flood of automobiles had changed the environment to such an extent that the unique flavor of the different communities had all but disappeared. My friend found in the bustling, clamorous cities that the leisurely pace of life was all but lost. Little streams had been polluted or funneled into culverts, destroying much beauty and charm. Traffic reaching all the way to the little back lanes made it difficult for people to walk.

In Tokyo, my friend flung up his hands and exclaimed that

he felt he had not left New York. But he said, hopefully, "Well, at least in Kyoto I should be able to recover some of the traditional Japan I loved." But, as I could tell from his furrowed brow the day he arrived in Kyoto, he had hoped for too much. Among other things, the city was overhung with smog. My friend sighed for the other, better days of his memory.

Later, though, as we approached my house we heard the ringing of the large bronze bell of the nearby temple. Every morning and night the sound of this bell reverberates through the neighborhood. It is a small sign that traditional culture has not entirely vanished. When he heard the deep mellow tone, my friend said, "I'd like to take that sound back to America."

WABI

TEA MASTERS HAVE OFTEN used poems for teaching certain concepts. An image or allusion in a poem would strike a tea master as approaching the meaning of a concept that was difficult, if not impossible, to explain. The poem, taken in its entirety, would then essentially teach by metaphor what was beyond direct explanation. *Wabi* is one such concept.

The foundation of the Way of Tea is based on the aesthetic of wabi, which sometimes has been translated as rusticity. But this aesthetic should not be confused with a love of the rustic. Wabi is a state of mind. It is better expressed by words such as frugality, simplicity, and humility.

How was wabi understood by the great tea masters of the past? Sen Rikyu apparently appreciated the following poem as representative of the tranquil state of mind one attains in the Way of Tea:

> As I look about,
> Neither flowers nor autumn-tinted leaves
> Near the grass-thatched hut

That stands alone by the shore.
The autumn dusk.

This scene, a solitary and humble hut, the landscape lacking any brightness of flower or autumn leaf, typified the total simplicity and quiet taste of Takeno Jo-o, from whom Rikyu had learned Tea. Rikyu himself, even as his own attitudes developed apart from his teacher's, continued to respect the feeling of wabi as expressed in this poem. However, at the same time Rikyu went a step further and developed a more vigorous response to nature than Jo-o, who identified the essence of Tea with the extreme plainness of nature.

In contrast to this, Rikyu pointed out another poem, which he felt most clearly revealed the spirit of wabi and the essence of the Tea he established.

To those who long for the
Flowers of spring
Show the young grasses
That push up among the snowy hills.

Rikyu was impressed by the intensity he found in the aspect of nature that continued to thrive and to endure, to renew itself endlessly; he found an example of this in the young grasses that, pushed down at winter by the weight of the snow, thrust upward with all their energy to peep through the snow.

The two poems quoted here both represent the state of purity and tranquility in the absence of colorful beauty, and both are settings of solitude. They may seem similar at first, but they are greatly different in that one represents the *yin*, or negative and ending, condition of things, while the other is the *yang*, or positive and beginning, state. It was Rikyu's comprehensive spirit that enabled him to understand that the Way of Tea encompasses both of these.

The Way of Tea has attained definition at the point where these two contrasting views merge to create that aesthetic criterion peculiar to Tea, the concept of wabi.

People seek flowers in full bloom; yet, while loving their beauty, we must appreciate the effort that brings these same flowers to full bloom. A tiny sprout pushes forth, knowing that it is spring. It has no choice; it must grow or perish. The truth of nature can be known from the life of a flower. Rikyu found this same truth in the Way of Tea. A person who has not experienced the rigors of austerity like the grasses cannot hope to understand the essence of wabi. It is only natural to appreciate the beauty of flowers in their season, but it requires a finer sense to uncover the beauty of the grasses beneath the snow. Rikyu knew that the state of tranquility and purity contains something dynamic and unquenchable; nature continually generates life anew. Rikyu identified this renewal and continuum with the essential element of wabi. It is this particular sense we want to cultivate and refine as we grow in the Way of Tea.

Sen Sotan, also called "Wabi Sotan," was invited to tea one day by the daimyo Nagai Shinsai. Since Sotan was considered a man of wabi, the daimyo prepared an extremely meager meal to serve Sotan. The next day, he called on Sotan to ask for his thoughts about the tea gathering. Sotan replied that while the experience was pleasant enough, he believed that, there being a style of tea suited for daimyo, the previous day's tea gathering did not suit Shinsai's position. It was a mistake to think that by affecting poverty he could achieve the ideal of wabi.

After a time Shinsai again invited Sotan to tea. Thinking that Shinsai must now understand wabi, Sotan brought along with him a poor plasterer. Among the many exquisite dishes served was the delicacy of freshwater carp. Sotan, noting how little the poor man ate, remarked to the plasterer that since he was unaccustomed to such feasts, there was no reason to feign indifference, and he should eat as much as he liked.

Neither the rich man nor the poor man could have understood wabi if they thought it required them to pretend to a state that was not their natural one.

INSUFFICIENCY

IT IS OFTEN SAID that when the economy prospers, the spirit becomes impoverished. Contemporary society may be very affluent, but this luxurious living seems the basis for many of our mistakes.

One important Buddhist sutra says that to escape from the eternal round of passions, desires, and suffering, and realize contentment, one must know one's limits. Only then comes the achievement of spiritual and material wealth, happiness, and satisfaction. On the other hand, those who do not know contentment, even though they should find themselves in heaven, will still continue to look for something better, envying the possessions and happiness of others. No matter how wealthy the discontented become, they will remain poor at heart.

In the beginning of the nineteenth century, a powerful daimyo wrote, "The original purpose of Tea has at its core the acceptance of the insufficient." The Way of Tea is a method by which one can come to accept and find satisfaction with one's lot in life. For example, by far the largest number of persons practicing Tea today no longer have access to a tea hut and gardens that have been specially designed and constructed for tea gatherings. But whether a tea gathering takes place in such a setting or not, the host must still direct his complete attention to the needs and comfort of his guests; his efforts must not diminish simply because of the absence of the "proper" qualities in the place where he serves tea. Meeting such insufficiency with creativity increases in direct proportion the depth of the experience of both the host and the guest.

Contrary to the belief that insufficiency is a source of discontent, Tea seizes that very insufficiency and builds upon it. The monk Ryokan said, "When you have a problem, face it; when you are sick, face it; when death stalks you, face it." To the enlightened Ryokan, it seemed obvious that when we face our difficulties we realize for the first time the shallowness of our complaints. It is useless to complain about one's lack of tea utensils or a place in which to serve tea. What may be at fault is our own inability to be creative with what is at hand. Use your own creative abilities and intelligence guided by the basic tenets of the Way of Tea and test your mastery constantly.

At the center of a life based on harmony, respect, purity, and tranquility is that inner peace that results from accepting one's limits and finding satisfaction within the incomplete. With this peace, dissatisfaction and anxiety vanish, replaced by self-possession and composure.

RESTRAINT

THE JAPANESE TEND TO ADMIRE tasteful restraint and to prefer inner profoundness to overt or ostentatious display. This is perhaps something with which the Japanese sense of beauty can be identified, something that can be isolated as an aesthetic attitude. Insofar as restraint of self-expression has been highly valued, direct expression of individuality has been regarded as naive, lacking in subtlety, or unrefined. It may seem contradictory, but this can be defined as "expression by the restraint of expression." For example, in a Noh play even the deepest of emotions is portrayed by a slight movement. In the famous screen painting of pine trees by Hasegawa Tohaku, the breath and life of the work lie in the unstated elements. The negative space of the painting is a testament to the artist's restraint. Musical instruments too, such as the *shakuhachi* and *biwa,* require and establish silence between sounds to give emphasis. Haiku poems cast a stone into water with the brevity of seventeen syllables, but the ripples extend endlessly into the reader's heart and mind.

Restraint produces energy or tension whose sources are the concentration of expression. The story of Rikyu and

Hideyoshi concerning the morning glories in the garden is a good example. The single flower preserved in the tearoom absorbed and greatly intensified the beauty of all the flowers in the garden.

In Japanese culture there are many examples of this capacity to express in extreme brevity what has been attained by the severest of discipline. The calligraphy of the Zen priest Ikkyu, the monumental simplicity and purity of architectural line of the Grand Shrine of Ise, and the austerity of a tearoom designed by Rikyu are three such examples.

Rikyu searched in the complexity of his times for the true meaning of Tea. It was within the vicissitudes of politics, war, and discord of every kind that Rikyu created a world of tranquility. He wrote:

> Tea is nought but this:
> First you heat the water,
> Then you make the tea.
> Then you drink it properly.
> That is all you need to know.

This was originally meant to caution against the corruptive and overindulgent practices of his day, and we who follow the Way of Tea must continue to put this simplicity into practice. It is necessary however, to keep in mind how long is the way to achieve simplicity.

The restraint that brings the wind to Tohaku's pines and places a single flower in the alcove can become part of our own lives through constant attention to the desire to heat water, make tea, and drink it.

TO THOSE WHO ASPIRE TO
FOLLOW THE WAY OF TEA

"To those who aspire to follow the Way of Tea, guard against jealousy. To place yourself at the center, to envy others, to tempt others—these are unpardonable. Know your duty, and as you immerse yourself daily in the Way of Tea, you will be rewarded with happiness. The more you look up to others, the clearer your own position in relation to them will become. Whenever something untoward happens, people try to make themselves look as good as possible. But if we remember the humble heart of the host in the tearoom, for he knows the spiritual taste of tea, then this persistent clinging to power for its own sake will be seen for what it is. Know what you know and know what you don't know, for only then will the limits of your strength become evident. To attain spiritual power, seize the chance when it offers itself; devote yourself to study and practice. In life are many who feign knowledge and lead others astray. No action can be more reprehensible. The Way is never exclusive. It is open to all to follow, but those who set out upon the path perforce need the help of those who have passed that way before."

My father left us these words, his reflections on human duties. They are timeless and applicable to everyone.

In my own hands I hold a bowl of tea; I see all of nature represented in its green color. Closing my eyes I find green mountains and pure water within my own heart. Silently sitting alone and drinking tea, I feel these become part of me. What is the most wonderful thing for people like myself who follow the Way of Tea? My answer: the oneness of host and guest created through "meeting heart to heart" and sharing a bowl of tea.

I have toured the world with the goal, "Peace through sharing a bowl of tea." Taking a bowl of green tea in your hands and drinking it, you feel one with nature, and there is peace. This peace can be spread by offering a bowl of tea to another. I hope you will drink and share this peace with me.

APPENDIX

THE FOLLOWING IS a transcription of a dialogue between Dr. Herman Kahn and myself that took place on the program "Cross Talk Japan" broadcast by Sun Television, Osaka, Japan, on October 13, 1978.

Dr. Herman Kahn is a world renowned futurologist. He is the founder, president, and director of the Hudson Institute, a nonprofit organization whose purpose is the study of policies for public benefit. He has published studies of the future of the world, utilizing data gathered at his institute, that reflect his faith in the wisdom of mankind and his broad knowledge. Recently he raised the question of Japan's growth in his book *The Emerging Japanese Superstate: Challenge and Response,* stating that the twenty-first century will be Japan's century. Some of his other books are: *The Next 200 Years* (New York: Morrow, 1976); *World Economic Development* (Boulder, Colorado: Westview, 1979); and, with co-author Thomas Pepper, *The Japanese Challenge* (New York: Crowell, 1979).

82

Sen: I feel very honored to have this opportunity to meet you. In the past you have given us worthwhile advice concerning our economic problems, particularly those related to Japan's economic growth. Today I would like to talk to you about the heart of the Japanese people, covering a broad range of Japanese traditions.

Kahn: I think we will naturally touch on the economy while we do so.

Sen: I wonder if we Japanese have forgotten the essence of being Japanese because we have been so preoccupied with things outside our country in recent years. This attitude makes me feel a sense of crisis for Japan as a nation, its economic position included.

Kahn: I am pretty much in agreement with what you have just said. We can think of two periods concerning this situation. One is when Japan's attention was focused outward, and it borrowed from the cultures of China, Europe, and the United States. The other is when Japan became introverted. The Japanese have essentially accomplished their aim of catching up with the West. So they are now in a situation where they lack a goal.

Sen: I think some unfavorable criticism of the Japanese, such as calling them economic animals, is due to the excessive efforts on the part of the Japanese to catch up with the Western nations. Under the rule of the Tokugawa shogunate, Japan went through a long period of isolation from the rest of the world. Then the Meiji Restoration [1868] took place before our country's stance toward foreign nations was clearly formulated. Western culture and traditional Japanese culture have existed side by side during the Meiji, Taisho, and Showa eras [1868–present]. I think certain national characteristics of the Japanese have been enhanced through this historical process. The Japanese have directed their attention both outward and inward. In your books you have strongly questioned how well the Japanese are aware of their own values. Would you like to comment on this?

Kahn: I think the situation is very close to what you have just said. I think the Japanese are returning to the traditional sense of values, though only partially. I think they are among the world's most remarkable people in that they fuse the Japanese and the Western sense of values. I think too much attention has been paid to the outside world, but wouldn't you say Japan is gradually turning back toward basic Japanese values?

Sen: I think that is true. Your advocacy of both technology and nature, citing gardens as a symbol, is impressive. I was very struck by your view that technology and nature unite, and their unification pushes traditional things forward. Will you elaborate on this?

Kahn: Japan has a population of one hundred and fifteen million. Affluence and technology are absolute necessities for all these people to survive. On the other hand, the Japanese have always lived in harmony with nature. Right now this harmony is disturbed. I think the Japanese are capable of creating a life style that truly unites technology and nature if they really try to regain harmony. This would serve to revitalize the traditional Japanese spirit, the Japanese heart, and the Japanese view of nature. I wrote in my first book on Japan that the whole country will become like a Japanese garden; I think this will become Japan's objective in many ways. Japan could accomplish a lot of things by accomplishing this objective. A very large undertaking, for example, a large-scale national land development, will inevitably require some sacrifice and some destruction. A famous economist, Joseph Schumpeter, called this "creative destruction." A part of the old must be destroyed in order to create something new. This doesn't mean all of it must go, but most of it will have to be destroyed.

Sen: I think that this kind of thinking is very important. In Japan, the term furyu has been in existence since the Heian period [794–1192]. I think furyu is a suitable term to express the serenity and resourcefulness of the Japanese mind. Furyu is written with the two characters, "wind" and "to flow," suggesting the flowing breeze. Therefore, one senses that something can be furyu while the breeze is blowing, but no longer furyu when the breeze stops. It is the same with economic expansion. Natural expansion takes place like a gentle breeze, naturally building on the strengths of various factors. But if the foundation is weak, what has been constructed can be destroyed at once by an unexpected happening, such as what happened during the oil crisis. Frantic scenes of people trying to recapture what has been destroyed are seen frequently in the political and economic arena of Japan today. I think this is due to the fact that Japan lacks what you call a unity of technology and nature.

Kahn: I wonder if the opposite isn't also true. What I mean is that as far as we can see, Japan's social problem is overconcern with basic security and insurance against adverse contingencies. Sometimes this results in excessive exporting of Japanese goods. Japan already has built a sound basis for economic security, but still is not quite self-confident. Up to now, Japanese energy was directed wholly toward improving technology and machinery, but now, for the first time since the Meiji Restoration, Japan has reached the point where it can direct energy to the marriage of technology and nature. Yet, Japan is still pursuing the old goals; it is a mistake.

Sen: Great leaders or successful men are not only involved with mechanical and rational things, they also concern themselves with what appear to be irrational or discursive elements. These are part of furyu. Take tea as an example. To have a cup of tea is very important to a Japanese. But everyone has forgotten the spirit behind serving tea. I think the time has come when leaders need to think back to the spirit of the Japanese traditions. I wonder if this kind of return to tradition substantiates your contention that the twenty-first century will surely be the age of prosperity for Japan.

Kahn: I agree with you completely. I would like to add only one comment: I don't think it was necessarily a mistake that the Japanese were totally preoccupied with machines and technology during the postwar period. It was all right up until recently. But isn't it going too far to continue it today? The time has come to change this emphasis, but it is always difficult to make changes. Japan did not become poor after the oil crisis but continued to maintain affluence in spite of it. Japan is still trying to keep on doing the same things. Beginning about 1968, Japan should have paid attention to things other than manufacturing plants and equipment. If it had done so, I think things would be much easier today.

Sen: In a way, Japan is an enormous conglomerate, top-heavy and with an unstable base. Japan needs to become balanced as a whole. It is said that this is the age of uncertainty, but I would like to stress that it is an age of instability rather than uncertainty. Certainly big, medium, and small businesses all play important industrial roles, but here big business is very powerful, notwithstanding the fact that small and medium-sized businesses comprise a large share of the industry. Therefore, there is a good possibility for traditional Japanese culture to be associated with the growth of small and medium-sized businesses. There is a strong desire on the part of the smaller businesses, even very stable ones, to become big business, and I think this kind of tendency on the part of business is irregular.

Kahn: That is right. Big, small, and medium-sized businesses all have different roles to play. All of them must be stable and must grow. I, too, think the role of small and medium-sized businesses will become important in the future. However, it is possible that they will face a very difficult situation during a period of adjustment. The distribution system in Japan is very complicated and costly. Somehow this needs to be reorganized. In the long run, aspects of both technology and nature need to be adjusted, as you said. I think it is important to direct this adjustment not only to suit production but also to improve the housing and other amenities of the Japanese people during the adjustment process.

Sen: Japan has become affluent, and the style of living in Japan has become standardized. As their life style changed, the Japanese have gotten away from living on tatami. Japanese think that living on tatami is stiff; in contrast, some non-Japanese think living on tatami is very comfortable and engenders a feeling of oneness. But many Japanese say tatami are uncomfortable, and they prefer a life style with tables and chairs. Our life style in itself is a mixture of different styles. Our meals are good examples. We will eat bread and drink milk for breakfast, eat Chinese noodles for lunch, and then have a Japanese-style meal with rice for dinner. Because we adopt so easily the life styles of others, visitors from foreign countries often ask us what has happened to the traditional Japanese life; what has persisted since the old days. What do you think about this?

Kahn: This is also a complicated problem. The eating habits of the Japanese have changed greatly. In a sense this is a very good thing. Generally, it has brought about good results. The Japanese are healthier and taller than they were before. On the other hand, Japanese gardens and traditional Japanese things are admired all over the world as symbols of serenity. It would be very tragic if these things should disappear from the hearts of the Japanese, as you say. But I don't think they are really lost. I think the Japanese will return to more of an appreciation of Japanese things in the year 2000 than today.

Sen: I don't think they are lost either. I am absolutely sure that the Japanese spirit will not be lost as long as the Way of Tea and other customs developing an appreciation of furyu continue to exist. I think the Japanese are undergoing a series of trials testing their ability to maintain their own traditions during a time of tremendous change. The first trial came following the Meiji Restoration, the second came after World War II, and now we are undergoing a third trial. In times like these we must be aware that we are Japanese and base our actions on that awareness. Otherwise, we may see non-Japanese studying and knowing more about Japan than we do ourselves. A hint of this odd phenomenon already exists. Would you like to comment on this?

Kahn: That is common in other countries also. But what you have just said contains a very interesting point. One must have self-confidence and be proud of oneself.

Even though Japan is a most successful nation, the Japanese lack self-confidence. It is wrong to feel hopeless about GNP or growth. Affluence is necessary in order to live comfortably in a small country like this. Japan has been very successful. The people have a longer life expectancy, and the problems of environmental pollution have improved. The important thing is not the size of the GNP, but to bring about the marriage of a high GNP and Japanese culture. Therefore, the Japanese should have confidence in themselves, as they have been more successful than the Western nations as far as industrialization is concerned. This is the biggest problem Japan faces today. The Japanese do not take pride in their remarkable achievements. They must take pride in themselves first and then view the future.

Sen: What you say is true. I think it is very important for the Japanese themselves to develop a sense of values concerning new things and traditional things, as you just said. Even among the Japanese, those who know little about it tend to reject the value of the Way of Tea, thinking that it is very strict, maintaining the stiff procedures of an old ceremony—that it is too formal. They say, "What's the use?" But the essence of Tea is to prepare a bowl of tea with sincerity and present it to a guest. In return the guest accepts it with gratitude. The Way of Tea teaches us the spirit of sincerity and gratitude. We Japanese will forget this sense of gratitude unless it is taught to us at home during childhood. I wonder if this tendency to move away from tradition will not result, gradually, in a tendency among the Japanese to lose sight of their own sense of values.

Kahn: I don't know much about the Way of Tea, but to place so much importance on a sense of gratitude, as you said, is a very Japanese attitude. Japan must return to the Japanese values. This does not mean Japan should forget about industrialization or industrial technology, but it ought to combine tradition, meaning, and formal manners with industrialization. This means building a new base on the old foundations and does not mean discarding the past. In this respect, I would be very surprised if the Japanese did not return to the Japanese sense of values—character, moderation, tradition, and formal manners. I rather think that this area is going to be strengthened in the future. Of course, I think it is the natural course to follow. Industrialization itself has been very good for Japan. But is it not the goal. It is only a means.

Sen: It is often said that we Japanese are very modest or very polite, but I think actually modesty and politeness are more natural features of the lives of non-Japanese. I think it is very interesting that terms like "after you," "excuse me," or "thank you very much" are used frequently overseas. When I go abroad, I notice that these terms are used in all kinds of places. I have tried to think of the same expressions in Japanese. When one drinks a bowl of tea in a tearoom, he will first say to the person sitting next to him, "Would you like to have this?" Then the person who was asked will say, "Please." This "please" has the same meaning as "after you." The first guest then drinks the tea, feeling gratitude in his heart. One is taught to be humble and polite through drinking tea in a tearoom. Basically, the Japanese have a sense of modesty and politeness. People overseas use expressions like "after you" or "thank you very much" very smoothly, but when a Japanese goes abroad, he cannot easily say *arigato gozaimasu* [thank you] or *sumimasen* [pardon me]. This might be because of the introverted nature of the Japanese. I think the Japanese must acquire expressions of gratitude, based on human nature, that can be appreciated by anyone if Japan is to have a place among the nations of the world.

Kahn: I agree with you, but the Japanese are a very polite people as a whole. At the same time they are very easily influenced by circumstances. Therefore, it appears that one of their characteristics is to change their attitudes and moral principles according to the situation. But from my own experiences, I can't think of any Japanese who does not know formal good manners.

Sen: Young people are often criticized as lacking in discipline, yet they have a hidden gentleness more than middle-aged or older people do. I think this is a worldwide trend; in today's world, East is no longer East and West no longer West. East and West are fast becoming one. Thus Japan's position is going to be very important in the near future.

Kahn: I think this is certainly a result of affluence. Life is very difficult and austere in poor and hopeless circumstances, and people must compete against each other. Under such circumstances it is difficult for everyone to be polite and friendly. It is also difficult to be tolerant. But there is no need for aggressiveness or avarice when a nation becomes affluent and an easier life comes in. In contrast, the Japanese have always possessed a sense of duty and moderation or self-denial. I suspect all this will gradually disappear as the Japanese become more affluent. I think that will be very sad. I hope that the Japanese will remain very affluent but live a moderate life, and not a soft life.

Sen: It is your view that Japan will have a more stable identity and hold a position of leadership in the world. Do you mean that this position will be supported by the Japanese placing more importance on nature, traditions, and a sense of values? I would like to re-ascertain this point.

Kahn: That is right. We can write completely opposite scenarios about this, but culture generally has two aspects: one is arrogance and the other is the reverse. The second is Japanese-like. It is bad to be dominated by humility. It will be very interesting to watch how the cultural identity of the Japanese will evolve in the future.

Sen: Traditionally Japan has had more intense exchanges with the United States than with any other nation. I believe these exchanges should continue. What should be done specifically toward this end?

Kahn: I don't think it is something that needs to be promoted artificially. The reason for this is that young people in the United States are very interested in Japanese things. Interests in a wide range of things from Zen to Sokagakkai [a Buddhist sect with its own political party] are increasing among young Americans. An interest in the language is one. Enthusiasm for learning Japanese is increasing. Wouldn't it be better to have a natural interest in each other and to have increased interactions arise spontaneously? Lately, Nichibei Kyokai [the Japan-American Association] is also placing a special emphasis on culture. It is good for governments to encourage it, but it is best when it occurs spontaneously.

Sen: I am very pleased by your saying that the Japanese should not lose sight of their spirit in the midst of economic growth. I am hoping that I may be able to help us keep our Japanese spirit in sight. Harmony between nature and technology, in its economic aspect, bears a relationship to the harmony we seek in the Way of Tea.

Kahn: That is exactly right. When a country is poor and trying to become affluent, life tends to be harsh, but things change when it becomes affluent. This is also true economically and technologically. It is important to be balanced from here on.

Sen: I am grateful for the opportunity I have had today to learn from you. It was like a floating breeze.

Kahn: The word furyu impressed me.

Sen: It is very fine that this was such a furyu meeting. I hope you will continue to be active for the world's sake.